395

DISCOVER YOUR ROOTS

A New, Easy Guide for Tracing Your Family Tree

by

Marilyn Markham Heimberg

Illustrations by Gary Todd

A  Book

P.O. Box 17120
San Diego, Calif. 92117

(714) 276-7171

ISBN: 0-918880-00-9

Library of Congress Catalog Card Number 77-77291

First printing 1977
Printed in the United States of America

Dedicated to

my dear parents

who endowed me with a priceless legacy

of caring, enthusiasm and self-reliance.

Acknowledgements

The faith and support of many special friends
helped to nurture this work into being. My deepest appreciation to Sharon, Bob, Jack, Shirley,
Garmin, Jeanette, Russ, Janet, Sandy, Vince and
Donna. Your encouragement, suggestions and crit-
iques were treasures.

Special thanks to my sons, Scott and Steve --
without whose understanding and "pitch-in" attitudes this book could never have been born.

A very warm thank you to Penny Feike, who shared
so unselfishly of her time and expertise. And to
Prentice Ford for his wisdom and guidance. Also,
to the many accommodating librarians, government
representatives and private individuals who
helped me dig out research materials.

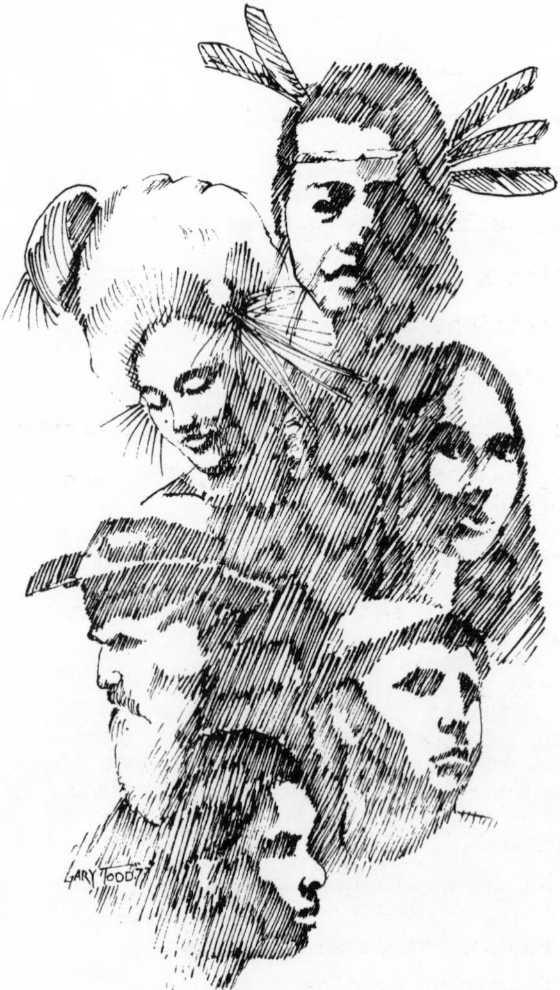
GARY TODD 77

Contents

1

Ancestor Hunting Can be Fun!

People will not look forward to posterity, who never look backward to their ancestors.

Edmund Burke

REFLECTIONS ON THE REVOLUTION IN FRANCE.

Vol. viii

There just may be a king or queen dangling from your family tree. Perhaps your forefathers possessed a castle, or a coat of arms. On the other hand, you could find several villains lurking in your closet. A distant relative may have been burned at the stake for witchcraft, or hanged for horse stealing. You'll never know... until you start digging!

Thanks to Alex Haley's dedication and creative skill, many more Americans are doing just that. ROOTS awakened family pride - an excitement about our heritage - a thirst to know of our beginnings.

The book you're reading is designed to help quench that thirst. DISCOVER YOUR ROOTS guides you through the underbrush and brambles of unfamiliar genealogical surroundings. Written in a new, easy format it leads you on a step-by-step safari through your ancestry. To embark on a genealogical journey is to do much more than begin a study of old, stuffy records.

First, it means becoming a detective. "If you like mysteries," says Dr. Thad Whalon, a university professor and avid genealogist, "It's much more fun to solve real ones in your own family." As a detective, you'll search for clues, developing your powers of analysis and imagination to seek out facts. Sewn and quilted edge-to-edge,

these discoveries create your family history. One
thing leads to another. That's part of the fasci-
nation, not knowing what might turn up next.

You'll also be an amateur psychologist. Once
you've found where materials are located, you need
tact and diplomacy to get people's cooperation.
You will employ common sense and intuition to
gauge where someone went or why they did a particular thing.

A new appreciation of history and geography
will emerge as you probe your forefathers lives
and destinations. Thinking through early life-
styles may even boost your understanding of
economic principles.

While you won't qualify to pass the Bar,
don't be surprised to find yourself becoming a
Legal-Eagle. You'll discover how to ferret out
secrets hidden in vital records.

Genealogy is ideal for anyone with an inquis-
itive mind. It is a fascinating hobby. And it
need not be expensive; the raw materials are in
every family. Tracing your ancestry has been
compared to eating popcorn: Once you get started,
it's hard to stop. Nourished to full bloom, this
pursuit can also become an engrossing occupation.
One housewife even parlayed her curiosity into a
title. She traced her Germanic name to a record
center in Bonn - and found she was a long-lost
baroness!

And family tree climbing is a marvelous
excuse for travel. More and more people are
planning their vacations to include a search for
their forefathers. What fun to discover great-
great Uncle Nathan really did come West during
the Gold Rush. Or to visit a historical site and
know that your blood relatives trod that same
ground years before. If you had a family who
were "doers" there will be a fantastic wealth of
intriguing material.

Genealogy is not a modern science. One
Egyptian King, Ramses II, traced his ancestors
back for 77 generations...and then had his family
tree carved in stone. The dukes of Luynes are
said to have displayed a picture of Noah entering
the ark carrying the Luynes genealogy. Noble
Elizabethans also claim they can include the ark
on their coat of arms.

And if you've ever investigated Swedish
history, you may have wondered why all the kings
called Charles are numbered VII to XIV instead of
I to VIII. That's easy to explain. In the
sixteenth century, the chronicler simply rein-

forced national pride by inventing six extra kings! A conscientious researcher must often pry fantasy from fact.

The Arabs and Jewish people kept carefully traced records of their genealogies in early times. The Celtic races in Western Europe assigned special officers to each clan. Their sole responsibility was to preserve the pedigree of the chief families. A "pedigree" is simply a recorded line of descent.

Among Anglo-Saxon races, however, little early attention was paid to the preservation of lineage. The first genuine effort to document family origins resulted from the feudal system and the growth of heraldry. In approximately the 16th century England's "College of Heralds" started visiting the various counties on a regular basis to record all genealogies where proof was available. But with the advent of improved parish records in about 1680, these visitations ceased.

Of course, learning the "facts" about our kin is only one facet. They weren't just a bundle of statistics. What's really fun is learning what they were like as people. Were they serious or jovial? Ambitious or lazy? Submissive or rebellious?

There is an intriguing new field of study that believes the more we know about our ancestors the more we know about ourselves. It views genealogy as a very "personalized" science. Dr. Mary Matossian, a history professor at the University of Maryland, is a leading exponent. She points out, "Americans have long prided themselves as being a nation of rugged individualists. But the truth is, most of us have derived our strength from our families. The more we know about our forebears the more we really know about ourselves."

Alan Haas explains this in an article in the May, 1976 issue of SCIENCE DIGEST. It contends that by plotting a psycho-history and looking for patterns of behavior from generation to generation, we can gain insight into ourselves and our present family ties. There may be a valid reason you're called a "chip off the old block!"

Reflect on your family. Is there a permanent, loving bond woven between members, or are relationships distant? And what about individual natures? Are you a decendent of feisty, rhinoceros-skinned men who often wore brass knuckles on

11

their tongues? Or were the males in your family
generally sensitive, intelligent and gentle?
What about the womenfolk? Delicate as dandelion
puffs? Oatmeal-like in personality? Or, strong,
dominant females?

Some family groups also excel in specific
areas. Take the Bach genealogy. It includes
more than thirty musicians and composers. Four
generations of Struves in Russia and the U.S.
contributed to the knowledge of astronomy. Al-
most a dozen Fries have been involved in Swedish
botany. And politics coursed through the veins
of several generations of Adamses.

People climb their family tree for various
reasons. Some because a fresh curiosity has been
unleashed. The question "Who am I?" prompts
their search. Others desire to establish eligibility for joining patriotic or hereditary
societies. Still others want to fulfill religious obligations.

Anita Cheek Milner, immediate past president
of the San Diego Genealogical Society, believes
that today's unsettled world has led people to
reach into the past for a feeling of security.

Families since Genesis have been officially
recorded through the male line. Therefore at
first glance, Genealogy may seem like a male-
chauvinist pursuit. This is not ture. We have
no intention of talking down to women. America
could never have been pioneered without the
strength and determination of women. Terms like
"forefathers" and "he" are used for ease in reading and understanding. They are meant to include
both sexes; not to demean the female gender.

In any event, when shinnying up your particular tree trunk, be prepared to encounter
scandalous information. You may tumble into
records you would rather not see. For instance,
G.D. found that a Civil War soldier-ancestor was
a deserter. And A.M. discovered that a great-
great grandfather had a provision in his will to
care for an illegitimate mulatto son. J.W.
found that one of her female ancestors was con-
victed of witchcraft in Salem, Mass. in 1692.

H.C. learned that one of her great-grand-
fathers walked out on his family. According to
a diary, one night he proclaimed he was going
outdoors to get a backlog for the fireplace.
Twelve years later he returned and announced,
"Here's that backlog." Do remember, though,
that no matter how negative the situation seems,
there is one redeeming quality: No man is com-

pletely worthless. He can always serve as a horrible example.

We hope, however, you will find DISCOVER YOUR ROOTS studded with good examples and practical help. While we have tried to be both basic and thorough, no one book could possibly contain everything about genealogy. It is suggested that beginning students read this Guide clear through once. Then go back and apply it in the order that feels best for you. Individual chapters have been organized to deal with the main elements of a genealogical search and created to stand alone...something you will never again do once you have traced your heritage.

2

How to Begin Your Safari

The brave are born from the brave and good. In steers
and in horses is to be found the excellence of their sires;
nor do savage eagles produce a peaceful dove.

Horace

CARMINA, Bk. iv

Preparation and focus are key elements in a successful safari, whether it involves a camera or a gun. To "bag" your desired genealogical game, you need a good start and proper direction. So here goes...

Begin with the most important person around: YOU! You are the top rung on this family ladder. Starting in the present with yourself, travel from the known back to the unknown. There isn't any mystery to working backwards. Take it a step - or generation - at a time.

INTERVIEW FAMILY MEMBERS

Living relatives are the foundation of your search. Through them you can sniff out clues like a hungry tiger, clamp your jaws down on the vital data, and drag it off to be happily devoured.

"Great!", you say. "But what am I looking for?" The information you seek falls into four main categories: names, dates, places and relationships.

It is best to start with the oldest members of your family. Those in their 70's and 80's will often remember things they heard as children. They may also have corresponded with other members or branches of the family. Try to learn where your ancestors came from and where they lived at given times. Knowing where they were located during the 1880 census will prove especially helpful later on.

```
┌────────────────────────────────────────────────┐
│           CAPTURE THIS INFORMATION              │
│                                                 │
│  NAMES            full given names (avoid       │
│                     initials)                   │
│                   any nicknames used            │
│                                                 │
│  DATES            birth, marriage, death        │
│                   if appropriate: immigra-      │
│                     tion, military service      │
│                     adoptions, migrations,      │
│                     divorces                    │
│                                                 │
│  PLACES           where born                    │
│                   where moved/migrated          │
│                   where died                    │
│                                                 │
│  RELATIONSHIPS    parents                       │
│                   spouse(s)                      │
│                   children                       │
│                   brothers & sisters            │
│                   close friends                 │
└────────────────────────────────────────────────┘
```

Don't just dredge up cold facts. Comb these old folk's minds for what your forefathers were like as people. Learn about their personalities, what they accomplished, the vocations they followed, what churches or groups they belonged to, how they suffered and who they loved.

It's a good idea to use a tape recorder when you are interviewing. The other person soon forgets about it and you're freed to really communicate and guide the conversation...rather than frantically taking notes.

Encourage them to talk about their childhood. Listen carefully. Try not to become fidgity if they repeat things. Just keep prodding with gentle questions and maintaining an attentive attitude. Meaty tidbits telling who, what, when, where and why are bound to slip out. It was from stories, key words and phonetic sounds passed on by his grandma, that Mr. Haley was able to begin piecing together the account of his family.

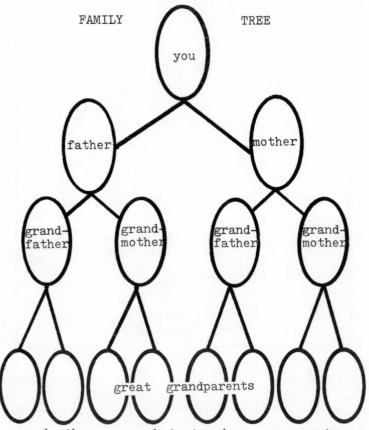

FAMILY   TREE

you

father   mother

grand-   grand-   grand-   grandfather   mother   father   mother

great   grandparents

Another approach to tracing your ancestry
is to establish a Family Organization. This is
simply an association of family members working
individually - yet in tandem - to develop the
line. By working as a team, the research is
speeded up. Another big plus is that it brings
the family closer together. It also avoids dupli-
cation of effort.

To start a Family Organization, make a list
of concerned people. Then write, call or visit
each. It is important to reach all these people
as one may have already performed research and can
save you much effort.

Here are tips on how to find "lost" living
relatives. One way through this thicket is to
address an envelope to their last known residence.

Boldly mark it with this wording: "Address correction requested - Do NOT Forward". The post office will then note on it any known address and return it to you for the huge sum of 25¢. You can also call the library and ask them to check phone books or city directories for the last known city.

If these snares fail to catch a lead, advertise in the newspaper in that locality for information on their whereabouts. Try placing an ad in that city or county's genealogical bulletins, or in the widely-circulated specialty magazine, THE GENEALOGICAL HELPER. For advertising information write Everton Publishers, Inc., P.O. Box 368, Logan, Utah 84321.

The next step in the Family Organization plan is to get everybody together for a reunion. At this exciting and important event you will no doubt meet distant cousins, nieces and nephews and learn of traditions and heirlooms you never knew existed. The group should set specific objectives and decide how best to carry out their research.

As you go about interviewing relatives and collecting information, remember one vital point. People sometimes garnish their recollections with sprigs of daydream and illusion. Or they pass on hearsay as "gospel truth". While this is usually done innocently, it is a poison dart for the genealogical researcher. An incorrect lead will send you scurrying along trails that intertwine and go nowhere.

Before you gulp down a strong dose of family tradition as fact - or blindly assume written data is accurate - be the devil's advocate. Accept it with reservation. Oil your search with logic and common sense. Do events match up? Is the chronological order reasonable? Is it possible for things to have happened in the way and time frame they supposedly did? Look for stories that corroborate each other. In a later chapter we'll show you how to validate what you are told by checking public records.

SEEK FAMILY DOCUMENTS

The other side of the contemporary family coin deals with locating objects and records to sprint you forward. Investigate old trunks and crevices in basements and attics. Be on the lookout for family Bibles, old diaries and journals, letters, newspaper clippings, scrapbooks, baby books, professional portfolios and account journals. Military papers, birth and death certificates, marriage licenses, divorce decrees, deeds and old photographs are also helpful.

Why do these items represent key watering holes on your safari? They often contain those good 'ole names, dates, places and relationships! Many photographers, for instance, marked their names and location on the back side of their work. This is an excellent clue if you are trying to discover where part of your clan lived. (And by checking census records, this tip may also yield a date.)

Of course, family Bibles contain references to births, marriages and deaths. Notice when the Bible was printed, as this establishes that all entries before that date were done from memory and therefore may be less accurate. Also note if the handwriting varies, thus suggesting that the book passed through several generations. Diaries also hold keys. Many jigsaw puzzles have been pieced together by reading through a diary with an eye for revealing genealogical information.

Now that you've armed yourself with both written and verbal ammunition, let's find out how to further use this arsonal.

3

Tips for First-time Adventurers

We cannot erase the bad records from our past.
                                        A. Maclaren, D.D.

Nor the good ones either, thank God.
                                        W. H. Howe

Now that you have harvested all those names, dates and places from home sources, it's time to start digging in public records. There is no unbreakable rule about exactly where or how to begin. Each family is an individual unit. You will follow the path indicated by the clues you have uncovered.

If you have the time, it's a good idea to get in on one of the many classes being offered in genealogy. These are typically sponsored by colleges, adult education groups or the Church of Jesus Christ of Latter Day Saints (Mormons). Another way to get excellent guidance is to join a nearby genealogical society. By attending their meetings and workshops, you'll be exposed to competent help and problem solving suggestions. But let's assume you are pursuing this on your own. What's the starting point?

Most U. S. towns or counties have some sort of depository that serves as a hub for genealogical records. It may be your local library, the county courthouse, a historical society, or even a genealogical society. These are the breeding grounds of your search. Go to them armed with all the data you have. The speck of information left at home because it seemed inconsequential, may be just the tip needed to break open whole new horizons.

And never be afraid to ask for help! While you can't expect others to do the actual search for you, don't hesitate to ask their suggestions for the best way to begin your individual adventure. Find out how to use the card catalogue and their filing and shelving systems. Learn what indexes are available to point you in the right direction.

To get firmly in mind what information you have - and make it obvious what gaps need filling - prepare a Work Chart covering four generations. It will take you through your great-grandparents and into history to generally the late 1800's.

PEDIGREE WORK CHART

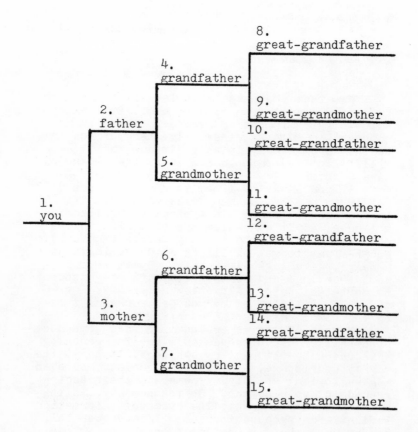

The individual's full name goes on the line. Then under each person, list the date born and where, the date married and where, and the date died and where. For instance, your father would look like this:

2. <u>James Neal HANKS</u>

12 May 1918
Chicago, Illinois
27 September 1946
Chicago, Illinois
6 January 1966
Miami, Florida

If you don't know a certain fact, leave a blank space as a reminder to locate that information. To avoid confusion, dates are always listed in the order of day, month, year. Each person has a number. Men are even; women uneven. This coding system is important. Later you'll probably want to create a Personal Profile Sheet[*] for each family member.

The Personal Profile Sheet will be cross-referenced by that person's number. Information on James Hanks will now always carry a number "2". On the Personal Profile Sheet you will capture all kinds of interesting things about Mr. Hanks - his occupation, brothers and sisters, accomplishments, personal philosophies, church and lodge affiliations, and so on.

Here are some tips to make your paper pilgrimage easier: Always print, rather than handwrite your chart. Librarians and future family members will be using it too. Use capitals for surnames (last names are called surnames). Always record women under their maiden names. If a person uses a nickname, list it in "quotation marks".

Be sure to write down information exactly as it appears. Don't alter it in any way. Customs and ways of recording were sometimes different in the olden days than they are today. You could change the meaning of something without even knowing it. It's also a good idea to record everything you find, even if you don't particularly need it. Someone coming behind you to trace the line may be delighted with a tidbit you found worthless.

There are two schools of thought about the best way to begin your search. Some say follow

[*]Available from Communication Creativity. See page 65.

only <u>one</u> line of the family. They feel if you start taking side-trips to trace aunts or uncles you'll end up lost in a tangle of material.

The opposing school believes you should work families by localities. They say if you are hunting in southern Massachusetts, track down any and every relative in that geographic area. Decide for yourself which approach to take.

It may be easier to start with your father's line as there wasn't as much documentation about women in the earlier years, especially from 1800 to 1840. Be sure to stick with the "blood line". Multiple marriages may require you to skip to the wife instead of the husband in some generations.

One of the basic things you will need to know is in which county a city is located. This can be gleaned from an atlas, a gazetter (a geographical dictionary), a postal directory or a map.

You may wonder how to leap the "generation gap" and move backwards - when you don't even have the name of your kin. Here's a sample of how you do it. Let's say you know your grandmother, Bertha Freshman, came from Roanoke County, Virginia. So you write the county courthouse there to get a copy of her birth certificate. This document carries her father's name. Presto! You have another generation. Much of genealogies excitement revolves around this kind of creative analysis.

Another treasure-trove is a collection of pamphlets for sale from the Superintendent of Documents, U.S. Government Printing Office, Washington DC 20402. They are called "Where to Write for Birth and Death Records" (HRA 76-1142), "Where to Write for Marriage Records" (HRA 76-1144), and "Where to Write for Divorce Records" (HRA 76-1145). You can purchase the trio for $1.05.

There are a couple of points about terminology you should know. Until the late 19th century the word "cousin" could mean any blood

relative except a brother, sister, mother or
father. And "brother" was often used to desig-
nate a brother-in-law, fellow church or lodge
member, or good buddy. So beware not to take
these titles too literally when you're researching that era.

One other oddity may cause you to think
you're seeing double. It is known as "double
dating" (Not the kind you used to do with another
couple). In early colonial American records
there are entries like 15 March 1750/51. We
could give you a long, complicated explanation...
but it is enough to know that our ancestors were
simply trying to catch up two different calendar
systems. The date means 1750 in the old calendar, and 1751 in the new.

Another morsel of advice for the novice is
never stop asking questions. Contact the Chamber
of Commerce, the Visitor and Convention Center,
ministers, local historians, postmasters, any
old-timers. You never know where a gem of knowledge is hiding. Unless you stir up the area
with inquiries, it may lie forever unnoticed.

Learning to ask the right questions also
helps in your correspondence. In addition to
writing family members, you'll want to contact
other individuals, societies and libraries concerned with the same family name or area. The
"Law of the Jungle" here is not to overwhelm.
Keep your letter to a single page and try to
confine it to only one specific question. If
you must probe several points at once, a practical approach is to ask the question - then leave
space for them to answer under it. Be sure to
tell what you already know to avoid time dupli-
cating information. Either type or use your
neatest handwriting.

Try to communicate on paper as you talk.
The idea isn't to impress them with your knowledge; but rather to get theirs! Use little
words and short sentences. Be conversational
instead of stilted. And do show appreciation.
Express your thanks in advance. Make it easy
for them to reply by including a stamped, self-
addressed envelope.

Record keeping is as important to genealogy
as patents are to an inventor. Happily, records
needn't be elaborate or confining. But remember
you will be exploring dozens of different documents. If you don't keep track of what you've
done and where information came from, your search
will lack direction and validity. Noone has

perfect recall. The source of information can scoot from your memory like a slippery bar of soap. So start right! Get a written handle on all data.

Simply set up a three-ring binder or note-book and log the source, where it is housed, the date and the person's number it refers to. Be consistent. And train yourself to write on only one side of the paper and to use full sheets rather than tiny scraps that are easily lost. It's a good idea to treat only one family per piece of paper. By thinking through your filing system in the beginning, you start out simply, yet effectively. As your family tree grows, your genealogical files will be orderly and easy to use.

4

Digging in County and

State Records

The evil that men do lives after them, the good is oft interred with their bones.

Shakespeare

JULIUS CAESAR

During one of Chicago's iciest days an elderly lady was observed trudging uphill gripping what looked like a walking stick. On closer observation it proved to be a plumber's helper. She would thrust the suction cup down at arm's length in front of her - walk up to it - then yank it up with a wet "woosh" and shove it ahead for another leg of her journey.

You, too, can be imaginative as you trek through the records of various government offices. By being resourceful you unleash a multitude of facts from such documents as birth and death records, marriage and divorce statistics, wills, probate records, deeds, tax lists and voter registrations.

One valuable resource tool is a service unknown to many people. It is the Federal Information Centers, a joint venture of the General Services Administration and the Civil Service Commission. There are 37 of these Centers perch-ed in major U.S. cities. Toll-free tielines feed to another 40 cities.

In addition to extensive federal government data, they also have information about state, county and city functions and personnel. They can tell you the names of whom to contact and provide phone numbers and addresses. When you need to know the best source for some data - or

are stymied about where to get certain knowledge -
try them. For a free brochure listing all the
Centers and tielines, write the Consumer Information Center, Pueblo, Colorado 81009. Ask for
brochure #621E.

Now let's look at county holdings. Record
keeping varies from place to place. To find out
who has what, check the HANDY BOOK FOR GENEALO-
GISTS. It is the "bible" for probing county
holdings and gives insight into migration patterns
and historical data for various localities.

When you arrive at the appropriate place,
approach a clerk to determine how documents are
arranged and indexed. Read the material for
genealogical clues. And remember to look under
all sorts of spelling variations on your Surname.

If you find conflicting data ask yourself
which version is most likely to be accurate.
Which was recorded nearest the event by the person
most likely to really know the facts?

Wills and probate records can help flush out
the skeleton of a family tree. These records
relate to the disposition of an estate after the
owner's death. They show relationships within
the family and often highlight outside, important
social links. They give the names of spouse,
living children and sometimes grandchildren. They
help you with localities by listing the residence
of the next-of-kin. Previous places the family
lived may also be mentioned. They give a time
frame, clues to land owned elsewhere, and often
show religious affiliations. Tune in to the
names of the executor and witnesses, as these
people may have contributed to shaping the anat-
omy of your family. One man learned of a devoted
friendship between his grandmother and a prominent
statesman by noticing a witness's signature on
the will.

Divorce records also glisten with potential.
They yield names and ages of children, the state
or county of their birth, when and where the
marriage took place, (ditto for its ending) and
often what the grounds were. Public records,
they are typically easy to get to and are normally indexed. For a small fee you can browse
to your heart's content. Other civil matters
that are recorded in court records are actions
dealing with orphans and guardianships.

Records of property acquisition and disposition can be good sources of genealogical data.
Early land records, ranging from private land
claims to homesteader's applications often indi-

cate where your ancestors formerly lived and for how long. Some of these earliest records, or copies of them, may be in the state archives. Tax records on real property show what land was owned and establishment in a community. Personal property which denoted slave ownership may hold a key for you.

The county seat of any county should have marriage certificates, deeds and other documents. But what if you come up empty-handed? Try branching out. What you need may be listed in an adjoining county. Your forefathers could have recorded vital particulars in a courthouse they passed through on the way to market or to visit a relative.

Expanding your scope still further, let's see what state records might offer. State Bureaus of Vital Statistics often record births and deaths. However, the majority of states didn't register such data until about the turn of the century. Some states also took their own census polls. These may be more detailed than certain federal censuses. We'll be exploring how to extract vital knowledge from census records in Chapter 7.

Local bodies can also shed light on the past human landscape. Ask around to find out who has custody of the vital records you need to investigate. Check with a municipal official like the city or town clerk.

5

Stalking Libraries for Fresh Clues

We can learn what to avoid from history's bad example,
and from her finest men we can learn what goals to
seek. But we are not warned of the dangers of inactiv-
ity because history does not record the story of those
who never tried.

Ellsworth Kalas

As a budding genealogist, you'll find that
you and libraries cling together like brand new
dollar bills. At the public library, for instance, a wealth of answers awaits you.

Again, it is paramount that you ask for
help. Before you can make use of these facilities, you need to know how card catalogs are
arranged and which indexes are available for
what purposes. Find out what collections of
books they have. Look at their vertical files.
Those are the metal filing cabinets that contain folders of clippings and booklets gathered
by subject. Some main branches also have special
Genealogical Rooms that yield a rich harvest.

Check in published books about families of
the same name as you. One excellent source is
the 48 volume AMERICAN GENEALOGICAL INDEX, edited
by Fremont J. Rider. He is also editing a con-
tinuation called THE AMERICAN GENEALOGICAL BIO-
GRAPHICAL INDEX. If you have a common name like
Jones or Johnson, admittedly it will be confu-
sing to know on which particular Jones family
tree you are a "twig".

To find the right clan, approach it like
a multiple choice test. Apply logic. Do the
ages, places and births match up with what you
already know? Toss out those that are obviously
wrong. Now push aside those that don't seem

right. Narrow your focus to the one or two
possibilities that are most likely to be correct.

Using this circumstancial evidence technique
you have fewer families to weed through. And
don't be discouraged if you come up empty handed.
Look how many times Babe Ruth and Hank Aaron
struck out. But that's not what they are remem-
bered for!
    If you are having trouble isolating a family
name, take a different route. Investigate the
geographical area. By reading about the town or
country where they were supposed to have lived,
you can pick up such intriguing clues as where
the residents who settled that area originated
from. Bingo! You have a lead on where else to
look for a possible family history.
    Newspaper files are invaluable in tracing
your lineage. They carry notices of births,
marriages and deaths. Community papers often
told of changes in family residence and notable
accomplishments of various members. The AYER
DIRECTORY OF PUBLICATIONS lists currently published newspapers. If you don't have luck there try
Clarence S. Brigham's HISTORY AND BIBLIOGRAPHY OF
AMERICAN NEWSPAPERS, 1690-1820 or Winifred
Gregory's AMERICAN NEWSPAPERS, 1821-1936, a Union
List of Files Available in the United States and
Canada.
    Major libraries also house collections of
telephone books. They are an excellent source
for finding if any relatives still live in a

given locality. By the way, these books can also be obtained from the telephone company.

Various indexes in the public library will make reference to works that are ideally suited to your search. While that individual library may not have the book or microfilm selection, for a tiny sum they can usually obtain it on a special-request basis from other libraries. Most records have been put on microfilm, or her more sophisticated sister "microfiesch".

The Library of Congress in Washington, DC also has material relating to genealogy and history. (Don't panic...you won't have to hop a plane to the nation's capital.) For a fee, if there are no copyright or other restrictions, the library's photo-duplication service will supply you copies of material in its collection. However, they cannot undertake actual searches. You must alert them to the specifics of what you want copied.

For detailed information about the holdings and use of the library, write the General Reference and Bibliography Division, Library of Congress, Washington, DC 20540. Ask for their free leaflets: "Reference Services and Facilities of the Local History and Genealogy Room", "Guides to Genealogical Research: A Selected List", and "Surnames: A Selected List of Books". Or call (202) 426-5537.

Some of the resources housed in the Library of Congress Local History and Genealogy Room include collections of American and foreign compiled genealogies, lists of passengers arriving in the U.S. and works on immigrations to America. It also contains periodicals - such as lineage books and lists of members of families - published by State historical societies, patriotic groups and hereditary societies.

Here you can find rosters of American soldiers and sailors who participated in wars in which the Thirteen Colonies and the U.S. were involved. And there are bibliography references to local histories that tell of early settlers, the establishment of local government, churches, schools, industry and trade. They also give sketches of community leaders. Elsewhere in the Library are collections of newspapers, city directories and maps that are relevant to your search.

The Daughters of the American Revolution (DAR) have a large geneological collection in their library. It, by the way, is appropriately

located at 1776 D Street NW, Washington, DC 20006.
You can reach them at (202) 628-4980. There are
over 90,000 books, pamphlets and manuscripts to
stalk in this library. They include copies of
entries in family Bibles and inscriptions on
tombstones, abstracts of court records, lineage
books, abstracts of Revolutionary War pension and
bounty land warrant application files in the
National Archives, and copies of church records.

For a dollar a day, non-members can make use
of this valuable collection any time except during
the month of April. It is entirely a reference
library and no material may be borrowed or rented.
However, they do have a copying and mailing service available. For details contact the DAR.

One of the main goals of the National Genealogical Society is to maintain a library collection of published and unpublished works. These
relate to genealogy, local history and heraldry -
which is the use of family insignia. Their library is located at 1921 Sunderland Place NW,
Washington, DC 20036. It is open to the public,
with a small fee for non members.

You may want to consider joining the Society
(details in Chapter 9) because members with U.S.
addresses may borrow most of its published materials by mail. The library also serves as a
repository for private collections of genealogical
books, papers and family histories.

By the way, here's a tip that can turn your
new pastime into a money-_saving_ venture. Con-
tributions of private collections are acknowl-
edged by the Society. Their letter can be used
to substantiate a charitable deduction on your
income tax returns!

Another marvelous place to shore-up your
research is the genealogical library system of
the Mormon Church. We'll be voyaging through
their holdings in the next chapter.

6

Expeditions into Church Collections

There is a moral and philosophical respect for our ancestors which elevates the character and improves the heart.

Daniel Webster

We will be exploring the records of many different churches in this section, but let's begin with the Genealogical Grandaddy of them all. The Church of Jesus Christ of Latter Day Saints (Mormons) maintains the world's largest genealogical research facility in Salt Lake City, Utah. It contains information on people from over a hundred countries and of every race, creed and nationality. The holdings amount to 150,000 printed volumes and over 1,500,000 one-hundred-foot rolls of microfilm.

Each day some 2,000 visitors roam through this genealogical forest, which reaches back even beyond 1538. In addition, the Mormon church maintains over two hundred branch libraries all over the world. Here you can borrow materials from the main library or arrange for copies. For a list of the branch nearest you, write the main library at 50 E. North Temple Street, Salt Lake City, Utah 84150.

According to an official church statement, the Mormons have been searching for their roots for seven generations. They call this feeling of family "The Spirit of Elijah." Those who follow this religion believe they must research the names and vital records of their ancestors in order to perform essential ordinances of salvation.

Their 180 microfilm teams travel the world to photograph records. With an average of 4,000 new rolls of microfilm processed each week, it is easy to understand why they own the world's largest collection of family records. Copies of these treasures are stored in vaults under 700 feet of solid granite in the Rocky Mountains.

A pilgrimage through their library holdings turns up such documents as land grants; deeds; probate, marriage and cemetery records; and parish registers. They also have a Family Group Record collection that indexes nearly 50 million names! What an ideal place to untangle the skeins of a family tapestry.

Other churches also have records that can clear away the fogs that may be clouding your search. If your ancestor belonged to a religious group like the Catholics or Episcopalians, you should be able to locate church records quite easily, as they belong to the Church. They are usually kept in books called "registers." Here you will learn of baptism or christenings that occured shortly after birth, records of actual marriages and burials, and names of family members.

Minutes of church meetings and activities often sparkle with helpful flecks of gold. Records such as membership rosters, admissions, transfers, lists of communicants and information about excommunications can establish names and movement of individuals.

If, however, your kin belonged to the Methodist, Baptist or a similar group, your quarry may be more difficult to pinpoint. These religious groups consider the records to be the property of the minister. Consequently, you'll have to locate where a particular minister's papers were deposited and check there. Often the family holds such records. Another lead is to investigate if this religious body sponsors a college, as information may be housed there. Churches have historical societies, too. Rochester, New York - for instance - is the home of the Baptist collection.

Information about the record holding of many leading denominations can be found in the October, 1961, or later issues, of THE AMERICAN ARCHIVIST, which is published quarterly by the Society of American Archivists. Another reference for locating church records is a CHECK LIST OF HISTORICAL RECORDS SURVEY PUBLICATIONS, cited under State and Local Records, which lists in-

ventories of church records in the States. A
SURVEY OF AMERICAN CHURCH RECORDS (2 volumes,
Salt Lake City, 1959-60) may also be helpful.
There is assistance available if you had family
members who left Pennsylvania in the early 1800's
in a Quaker migration to Ohio. For all major
Quaker congregations in the U.S., check the
ENCYCLOPEDIAS OF AMERICAN QUAKER GENEALOGY.

7

Tapping Census Information

My name may have buoyance enough to float upon the
sea of time.

Gladstone

If you are convinced that a certain ancestor
was brought by the stork and dropped into nowhere - census records can come to the rescue!
Census schedules help you establish other family
members and fasten your search to a specific
locality. For a list of what items are contained
in each, see Appendix A.

The first census was taken in 1790. It is
a marvelous "finding tool" because it has been
indexed and published. What this means is that
with simply the name of a person likely to be
a head of household during the late 1700's, you
will be led to the proper census records. In
turn, they reveal the county in which the family
lived and identities of all free white males and
free white females who resided in that household.
Thus, you find links to spouse, children, and
perhaps parents. The 1790 census also listed
slaves and other persons in a household.

This 12-volume index is called HEADS OF
FAMILIES AT THE FIRST CENSUS OF THE UNITED STATES
TAKEN IN THE YEAR 1790. It can be found in most
major libraries.

Once you learn the number of the microfilm
roll, you can request it from the closest branch
of the National Archives (more about them in
Chapter 8), Mormon genealogical libraries, or any
public or college library that has microfilm

reading machines.

Federal census takers have spun statistical webs every ten years since 1790. In general, the schedules through 1880 are open to the public. Unfortunately, only remnants remain of the 1890 records. Most were destroyed by fire. The 1900 records are open to family researchers at the Federal Records Center, the National Archives and branch archives.

The 1850 records are festooned with especially important information. They were the first to contain the age and birthplace of each family member. They carry facts about race, occupation, literacy, sicknesses or disabilities. Supplemental schedules for slaves may also prove revealing.

When you think through the data contained in the 1850 census, you can often develop a pattern to serve as a catalyst for your search. Let's suppose that your forefather was Ruther Atwood and he was 55 years old when the census was taken. You learn he was born in Maryland, but was renumerated in the Boone County, Missouri census. According to the census records, his wife Faith Browne was born in Virginia. Their children's birthplace is listed as Missouri.

From this you deduct that his wife's family probably moved from Virginia to Missouri prior to their marriage. The two families must have lived in close proximity for the romance to spring up. And since the children range in age from 1 to 16 years, you know this Atwood clan has a stable background in Missouri. By analyzing information and piecing the items together, you can draw a family portrait that is both accurate and revealing.

Beginning in 1910, records became confidential by law. Census records are collected for statistical purposes only, and are - therefore - exempt from the requirements of the Privacy Act of 1974. Generally, the U.S. Census Bureau releases information for this century only to the person, his or her heirs, or a legal representative.

Under certain circumstances, and depending on the particular item requested, some contents may be released. Applications for information

can be mailed to the Bureau of Census, Personal
Census Services Branch, Pittsburg, Kansas 66762.
Questions concerning the availability of publish-
ed statistics may be directed to the Bureau's
Data User Services Division, Customer Services
Branch at (301) 763-5045.

Before we leave the census taker's baili-
wick, one other point deserves mention. A number
of State and territorial censuses were taken,
particularily in the 19th century. These are
outlined in THE UNITED STATES CENSUS COMPENDIUM.
It was published by Everton in 1973 and includes
much recently located documentation.

8
Making Friends with the National Archives

Sence I've ben here, I've hired a chap
to look about for me
To git me a transplantable an' thrifty
fem'ly tree.

- Idem BIGLOW PAPERS:
2nd Series, No. 3

As the exciting voyage through your origins pushes forward, you will want to become acquainted with the National Archives and the National Records Center. These are America's historical treasure houses. With holdings that date back to 1716, they capture the sweep of the past.

The National Archives Building is in Washington DC; while the Washington National Records Center is in the nearby suburb of Suitland, Maryland. There are 11 regional archive branches scattered throughout the country. For a list of locations and areas served, see Appendix B.

If your search has previously poked along like a car running on only two cylinders, here is where it gets the needed power boost. The genealogical "finds" here are so hot they should be written on asbestos. There are pension records, steaming with names, dates, places and relationships. Ships' passenger lists - cargo manifests - Indian tribal data - military service information - guardianship papers - land records - all pulse with clues.

And if you don't live near a regional branch, you can harvest much of this information through the mail. Photocopies of most records will be supplied for a moderate fee.

Now let's wander through some of their holdings to find out more specifically what is available.

Land records are criss-crossed with bounty land warrant files, donation land entry files, homestead applications and private land claim files. By sifting through the donation land entry files and homestead applications, for instance, you can learn the following: Name of applicant, location of the land and date it was acquired, previous residence or post office address, age or date and place of birth, and marital status. But it doesn't end there. More "goodies" are contained in such records. If your forebearer was married, the given name of his wife, or size of his family will be noted. If he was of foreign birth, evidence of naturalization or an intent to become a citizen is listed. Supporting documents show the immigrant's country of birth and sometimes even the date and port of arrival!

Naturalization Records are here, too. The National Archives has photocopies and indexes of these documents from 1787 to 1906, filed by courts in Maine, Massachusetts, New Hampshire and Rhode Island. For proceedings of the District of Columbia, 1802-1926, the Washington National Records Center is your source.

Customs passenger lists and immigration passenger lists of ships arriving from abroad at Atlantic and Gulf of Mexico ports are found here. Monitoring custom passenger lists yields such information as name, age, sex and occupation of traveler; the country of origin and the country to which the person was going. And if an individual was born or died in passage, the date and circumstances are noted.

Passport applications can be helpful factfinders. The archives has these applications and related papers for U.S. citizens who sought to travel abroad between 1791 and 1905. They will make limited searches for age and citizenship in such records that are at least 75 years old.

Personnel records may also aid in your detective work. If Grandpa Pohle was a civilian employee of the Federal government and his service ended before 1910, sleuthing through these files is smart. (Personnel records for most civilian employees who terminated after 1909 are in Civilian Personnel Records - GSA -, 111 Winnebago Street, St. Louis, Missouri 63118).

Of course, only certain information can be released from Federal employee records. It is limited to names, position titles, grades, salaries **and** duty stations.

Service records for the Army, Navy, Marines and Coast Guard are housed in the Archives. Anytime you are requesting data on a service man be sure to include his name, the name of the war in which he served and the approximate dates. We'll talk more about military records in Chapter 10.

Claims for pension and bounty land - even if they were not approved - may resolve some of your family mysteries. They would be filed in the name of the veteran. These claims are requests for a dole of money or land which was awarded to the veteran or his widow and other dependents.

Indian records are arranged by tribe. Archive holdings deal mainly with the Cherokees, Chickasaws, Choctaws, Creeks, and Seminoles from 1830 to 1940. They are rich in detail. You can find out about annuity pay rolls, Eastern Cherokee claim files, names of family head, number of persons in a family by age and sex and description of property owned before removal.

There may be dates of departure from the East and arrival in the West. Sometimes both Indian and English names are noted. Any head of household who was at least one fourth Indian was listed in these records, so even if you have only a little Indian blood - this may be another path to follow.

Help for Blacks trying to discover their history can also be found here. The state department has recorded selected records relating to the Negro in U.S. military service from 1639 to 1886. Ask for microfilm publication #T-823.

Records of the Bureau of Refugees, Freedmen and Abandoned lands are also on file. For them, you want group 105. By serving in the Revolutionary War, it is estimated about 5,000 Blacks won their freedom.

Additionally, a collection of miscellaneous tidbits await your investigation. Births, marriages and deaths at U.S. Army facilities during the period from 1884 to 1912 are catalogued. There is a card index for the Virginia 1810 census. And an index to the 6,160 names surviving on the 1890 schedules.

Various gems are lodged in the records of District Courts of the United States. Try prospecting through their criminal, civil, admiralty and bankruptcy dockets, files and indexes. You may unearth profitable veins by studying lists of jurors, names of court officers, litigants and their attorneys, or witnesses. Of course, this is an ideal place to dig up a family "rascal"... which makes for fun story-telling.

Now let's peer through the doors of the regional branches for a moment. While they serve as a funnel for the main facility, and can tap it's vast storehouse of knowledge, they also have unique characteristics. As an example, if your descendants lived in Samoa, you would want to investigate the San Francisco depository. The 1899-1965 records of the Government of American Samoa are kept there.

Seattle serves as home for records of the Office of the Governor of Alaska for 1884-1958. And the Los Angeles facility contains Forest Service records that include grazing permits, oil permits and mining claims.

It is impossible to outline all the information available in the Archives. There is a free pamphlet, however, that will give you more details. Write the National Archives and Records Service, General Services Administration, Washington DC 20408. Ask them for general information leaflet #5, "Genealogical Records in the National Archives."

You can also talk personally with research consultants by calling (202) 523-3218. These experts will direct you to the proper sources and offer suggestions for solving thorny problems.

9

Help from Genealogical Societies and Publications

We are the children of many sires, and every drop of blood in us in its turn betrays its ancestor.

Ralph Waldo Emerson

Genealogical societies and publications are woven together like the warp and woof of a fabric. Both are immensely helpful to the person trying to shake loose new branches on their family tree.

The National Genealogical Society is located at 1921 Sunderland Place NW, Washington DC 20036. Their express purpose is to promote nationwide interest and scholarly research in geneology. Their emphasis is three-faceted: Meetings, library and publications. You may want to consider joining this organization as several research tools are available to members. (Annual membership is $20).

They publish a Newsletter and the NATIONAL GENEALOGICAL SOCIETY QUARTERLY. The Quarterly has carried thousands of records and many articles on families and locations of source materials in all parts of the U.S. and foreign countries like England and Germany. They also run "ancestor hunting" ads. The society issues special publications dealing with such varied topics as migration trails east of the Mississippi River - Lancaster County, Pennsylvania tax lists - medieval English records - heraldry - and genealogical research in German-speaking lands.

For an up-to-date list of all societies, libraries and professional genealogists, consult the July-August issue of THE GENEALOGICAL HELPER.

This is the most popular publication on the subject. It is distributed six times a year by Everton Publishers, Inc., P.O. Box 368, Logan, Utah 84321. Most large libraries have a copy, or you can subscribe for $13.50 a year.

A handy surname index refers to all names listed in each issue. There is a locality and subject index in each issue, too. A new feature, starting with the May-June 1977 magazine, is the "Bureau of Missing Ancestry." This directory contains listings from genealogists all over the world. Of course, each HELPER overflows with ads from people seeking new twigs on their family trees.

To learn of other genealogical publications, check ULRICH'S INTERNATIONAL PERIODICALS DIRECTORY. It is a standard reference work available in most libraries.

There are countless thousands of people interested in tracing their lineage. In fact, this is the fastest growing hobby in the United States today. Be sure to look through the advertisements in genealogical publications to see if you can find someone working on the same family. Even if they are working on your name, but not your actual family, it's beneficial to affiliate with them. And watch for those interested in the same general locality. Chances are they may tumble onto facts that will speed your research. An added bonus, this is a fun way to meet new friends.

There are certain book companies that specialize in family history books. Most of these are printed in very limited numbers. Therefore, they quickly rank next to first editions or rare books...more likely to go up, than down, in value. If you discover one that relates to your ancestry, grab it! You may not be able to find a copy later.

If you are really stymied, or can afford to speed up and "professionalize" your search, assistance is available. You can obtain a list of professional researchers who, for a fee, will trapse through libraries, archives and court records for you.

For one list, write the Board of Certification of Genealogists, 1307 New Hampshire Avenue NW, Washington DC 20036. They request a dollar contribution be included to defray the costs of printing and postage.

The Mormon church at Salt Lake also lists professional genealogists. They have strict

requirements for those who become Accredited
Researchers. These professionals must log 1,000
hours in LDS church records, another 1,000 hours
in their area of specialty (midwest states, Scan-
dinavia, etc.) and must pass a 10-hour examination with a 95% accuracy rate.

10

Marching Through Military Records

What is past is prologue.

Shakespeare
THE TEMPEST

Willing, active battalions of military information stand ready to respond to your commands. If you've discovered that a forefather served in any war fought by the United States, various service and veteran benefit records may contain facts about him and your family. By drafting them into your search, you can win additional genealogical feats. Military records are also valuable in establishing eligibility for patriotic societies.

If your search is bogged down at the moment and an ancestor - or close relative of his - lived at a time when he might have served in a war, it makes sense to go ahead and investigate the appropriate war.

A summary of an ancestor's service and subsequent benefits can usually be obtained from the National Archives by providing certain information in your mail query. You will need to supply the name of the person, approximate dates he served (or at least which war) and the state where he enlisted. If known, also include his regiment or, in the case of a Navy enlisted man, the name of a vessel he served on. If he fought in The War Between the States, tell whether he represented the North or the South.

The Federal Archives has U.S. Navy service records up to 1885; Army records for enlisted

personnel up to November 1, 1912, and for officers up to June 15, 1917. Their Marine Corps
records go up to 1895. Service records for
persons who served in predecessor agencies to
the United States Coast Guard run from 1791 to
1919.

Records for after these dates are in the
National Personnel Records Center, Military Records Division, 9700 Page Boulevard, St. Louis,
Missouri 63132. When you write them ask for
standard form 180.

Statistics relating to volunteer soldiers
who fought in various wars from 1775 to 1902 are
also housed in the National Archives Building.
Although they are of little genealogical help,
they are valuable for proving military service.

Regular Army service records, on the other
hand, are an abundant source of genealogical
data. These registers of enlistment show each
man's name, age, place of birth, date and place
of enlistment, regiment and company. They also
note his occupation at the time of enlistment,
give a physical description, and summarize the
date and reason for discharge. Where applicable,
the date of death or desertion is also included.

There is one catch. Only those records over
75-years-old are in the public domain. "Younger"
records are restricted to the veteran or their
immediate next of kin. Telling you about these
trophies, then saying you can't get to them is
like giving panty hose to a mermaid. Right?

Wrong! Just because certain records can't
be made available to the public, or copied in
their totality, doesn't necessarily mean they
are under wraps. Information from them will
normally be furnished legitimate searchers on
request.

Foraying through veteran's benefit records
will trigger more results. As an inducement to
serve, free land or monetary rewards were the
order of the day. From the earliest times of
English settlement in America, the Colonies gave
financial aid to persons disabled in military
service and to dependents of persons killed in
wars. This took the form of pensions or bounty
land claims, which were public land grants for
military service.

Pension files relate to claims based on
service in the Army, Navy, or Marine Corps between
1775 and 1916. Notice that this covers not just
pensions granted, but also any applied for. Documents submitted in support of some pension claims

include affidavits attesting to service, pages
from family Bibles (a super source for "goodies"),
and copies of birth, marriage and death records.
For service in the Civil War and after, a file
may also include Bureau of Pensions questionaires,
which contain more genealogical gems.

If the veteran himself applied for a pension
or bounty land warrant, the file usually shows
his age, or date of birth, and place of residence.
If his widow made the application, the file shows
her age and place of residence, her maiden name,
date and place of their marriage, and the date
and place of his birth. When an application was
done on behalf of minor children or by heirs of
the veteran, their names and sometimes ages or
dates of birth are shown.

The booklet, "Military Service Records in
the National Archives" goes into greater detail.
You can get a free copy of it from the Publication Sales Branch (NATS), National Archives,
Washington DC 20408. Ask for leaflet #7.

State records may also hold promise for you.
Some have files of military service performed in
state or colonial units. Such records are often
deposited in the state archives. Try the State
Adjutant General's Office in the state capital.
For information about Confederate pension application files, write to the appropriate official
in the capital of the state from which the service was rendered, or where the pensioner resided
at the time of his death. The Morman Library in
Salt Lake has state indexes and a consolidated
index to Confederates.

11

More Sources and Ideas to Enrich Your Journey

The man who has not anything to boast of but his illustrious ancestors is like a potato - the only good belonging to him is underground.

Sir Thomas Overbury
CHARACTERS (1614)

We need to approach our genealogical hunt with imagination and flexibility, much like the German shepherd dog who tried to take a bone away from a Chihuahua. The Shepherd rumbled a ferocious growl, bared his fangs and did his best to threaten the smaller dog into dropping his treasure. But the Chihuahua stood firm. So the larger animal tried a different approach. He simply picked up the smaller dog - bone and all - and trotted away.

Now that's creative thinking! And if you can climb out of the usual habit pattern and approach your research from fresh angles, you too will trot away with new treasures.

Let's say, for instance, you're trying to determine the approximate date an old letter found in an attic was written. Did you ever think of looking at the denomination of the stamp as a solution? By checking when that amount of postage was necessary to mail a letter of that weight, you can probably isolate the period.

And have you taken a really close look at the old "sampler" great, great Aunt Bertha embroidered when she was a mere girl? It just might contain the names and ages of her brothers and sisters. The date of her work may also be included.

What about that family heirloom you've been

thinking about resilvering? Did you look it over
for the original owner's initials, or a company
name that might help you establish an identity or
date? Have you conferred with antique dealers to
see if they can shed any light as to where or when
it might have been manufactured?

By using common sense and stretching our
minds to peek around the obvious, new solutions
appear. We can avoid hardening of the attitudes.

Now let's probe some miscellaneous traps that
may momentarily ensnare you.

Should you find a "bound" child in your ancestry...that means the youngster was in an or-
phanage or was bound out by his or her mother
because the father was killed in the Civil War
and there was no way to care for the child. The
best method to uncover information about such a
person is to roam through local records in the
community of the foster parents.

What do you do if you locate a family Bible
brimming with information...only to find the owner
of the book will not release it to you? One way
around this problem is for both of you to go
together and have a photocopy made of the vital
data. Then get an affidavit from the person and
have it notarized.

Suppose you're trying to get a fix on a
locality, but none of the prevailing family records helps to establish the place. Scan everything for names of famous people in history who
might have been friends of your relatives. The
travels of a VIP are much more easily tracked;
chances are good the dignitary and your family
were in close proximity.

Many helpful hints rest under the canopy of
death. Newspaper obituary notices can be as
valuable ruling <u>out</u> a clan as they are providing
substantiating evidence. Maybe you've been concerned that you don't have the correct "Kingsley"
family. You read in the obituary notice the only
surviving daughter is named Mary. But the information you have indicates the deceased would have
three daughters...all with very different names
and all alive and well. You've just lassoed a
big find. Currently published newspapers are
listed in the AYER DIRECTORY OF PUBLICATIONS,
which is in most large libraries.

Local undertakers and cemetery records bris-
tle with information. But don't forget that a
funeral director's files are private. You could
be denied access. This is a good place to use
tact and charm so the director will want to

cooperate in your project. It's worth the extra effort. These records give the date your ancestor died, names of the nearest relatives and the place of burial. A polite letter usually yields the desired results.

Once you're armed with the place of burial, new vistas open. Gravestones and monument inscriptions carry messages about date and place of birth, names of parents, spouse, place of marriage, names of children, sometimes even religious affiliation, lodges and military service. And look around the cemetery. Related people were often buried on the same lot, so you may find more connecting branches. It's a good idea to take along some spray talcum when you go on such safaris. The inscriptions are often eroded and a light squirt of talc brings out the old lettering.

Genealogical researchers sometimes use this cemetery technique to backtrack. Once they have the date of death, they go to the local newspapers following that date to find the obituary. It's a sad commentary that most of us get the best write-up of our lives when we die!

The customs, religion and race of our ancestors are also important genealogical keys. In the New England colonies, for instance, whole groups of settlers moved from established colonies into the wilderness to found new ones. Therefore, vital town and church records are few. Virginia townfolk...on the other hand...established more permanent residence, so their records are in family archives, at county seats and in the scattered county parishes. And the restless pioneers from the middle states, especially those outside the large towns, immigrated to the West. It's a real challenge to find public records to validate their comings and goings.

The Mormons settled in Utah. Some Quakers settled in New England; others migrated from New Jersey to Pennsylvania, and eventually settled in Ohio and Indiana. Knowing that your pedigree contains people of these faiths gives you a hint of where to look for them. Should you be of Jewish descent, check the American Jewish Archives, 3101 Clifton Avenue, Cincinnati, Ohio 45220. FINDING OUR FATHERS by Dan Rottenberg is a good how-to-do-it book for tracing Jewish ancestors.

If you are of Indian blood, the U.S. Government Bureau of Indian Affairs has a wide variety of helpful records. These include birth, marriage and death certificates, registers, tribal census records, school records and correspondence files. The National Archives and it's branches also have various reservation records and information about Indian estate and allotment records.

Blacks may find help from the Kinte Foundation, located in the National Press Building, Washington DC 20004. It is a clearing house for Black genealogy and contains such materials as slave chip cargo manifests, announcements of auctions, bills of sale and plantation records.

12
What's in A Name?

A man's name is to him the sweetest and most important sound in the English language.

Dale Carnegie

HOW TO WIN FRIENDS AND INFLUENCE PEOPLE

Your name...first, middle and last...may unlock many keys to your origins. And the tags your ancestors wore can shed light on what country they came from, where they lived, what they did, their social status, physical appearance, their individual personalities, personal idiosyncracies - what they were really like as people!

Sound impossible? Well, it's not. There is much more behind a name than most of us realize.

It is a very important possession. Don't you feel a certain resentment every time someone wants to identify you by your social security number or drivers license number? Our name says who we are. It is as personal as a toothbrush. To deprive us of it is to impersonalize and dehumanize us.

Thousands of years ago, people only had first names because there was no mass communication or way to travel far. You only needed to remember a handful of people in your community. But as civilization grew, it became necessary to develop a way to distinguish one John - or Joan - from another. Our European ancestors seem to have queued up in four major lines when it came to creating a descriptive surname.

One team tacked the term "son" on the end of the father's first name. Thus, William's son became "Williamson", Jack's son was dubbed "Jackson", and so on. Some German names end in "sohn", Scandinavian names may conclude with "sen", Armenian's use "ian", while Russian and Servian endings are "ovitch". The flip side of the coin is represented by the Irish and Scot's, who denote son by beginning their names with "Mac". The Irish "O" stands for grandson.

Females also played on this team. From Norway we have Lavransdatter, meaning the daughter of Lavran. And Iceland produced women named Gunnarsdatter and Kristinsdatter.

Another team used occupations to guide their selections of last names. This is where we get the Shepherds, Potters, Knights, Taylors, Carpenters, and Lockmans. If your last name is "Farmer" it's a distinct clue about a distant generation. Likewise, if you are a "Steward", your ancestor no doubt did the Lord's bidding. If you're a "Parkman", your progenitor was a gamekeeper in charge of a park. Many who chose professions or vocations for their names came from small villages in Europe.

People on the third team were named after places. If your family owned a manor, village or castle, their name may have matched it. And for many, topographical elements spawned their names. If your family lived in a rocky area, the last name might be "Stone." Samuel "Hill" came from hilly terrain; while George "River" resided by flowing water. If you are a "Pool", a "Brook" or a "Clay", this is your group. A suffix indicates approximation to a certain natural feature, such as Edward Overhill or Thomas Atlake.

Those who found themselves on the fourth team were tagged with a nickname that related to either the way they looked, what they were good at, or a personal mannerism. Those names - given by others - often stuck. Long, Little and Stout were based on appearance. William Fish was a good swimmer; while James Fox was sly and crafty. And poor Louis Hogg must have been deemed very dirty or greedy by his neighbors.

Names also offer hints on social status. It is logical to reason that if your forefathers took a name Shoemaker or Cook, they were of the working class. On the other hand, a German name like von Hindenburg means from Hinden Castle and denotes social and economic prestige.

Another interesting point is that the prefix "Mister" did not originally apply to every man. Only those who were considered gentlemen (the landed gentry), clergy or a man in high civil office used that term. Likewise, "Mrs." did not have today's connotation. It wasn't used to signify a married woman, but rather to denote social status. Mrs. was simply the feminine equivalent of Mister.

Of course, many names changed. Sometimes this was done intentionally by the owner; other times it just happened. Since few people could read and write in the early days, just the passage of time was responsible for some changes as names went through phonetic corruptions. Several foreigners' names were altered by customs officials. When the immigrants came in at Ellis Island in New York harbor the customs people could not always understand their names - so they shortened or "Americanized" them.

During the 17th and 18th centuries when Europeans came to the U.S., they frequently found their names added to communication barriers. Anglo-Saxons simply couldn't pronounce them. So the German Zimmerman and the Greek Marongopoulos translated their names to the American "Carpenter". The Italian Zannini translated to "Jennings" and the Polish Piezarz became "Baker." A Finn by the name of Kolehmanen became "Coleman." A Jewish man traded his Tofilovsky for "Tofield."

Spelling was also responsible for some name changes. For instance, census takers spelled the common name "Brown" seven different ways in the 1790 census! And one woman who was trying to trace the name of Meriwether found that one branch of the family had arbitrarily added on "a" to make it Meriweather; while another branch doubled the first "r" to spell it "Merriweather." For this reason it is especially important to consider all possible variant spellings when climbing your family tree.

Circumstances sometimes kill names. Many African family names were doomed when Blacks were stolen into slavery and assigned names on plantations in the New World. As they were sold, new owners sometimes gave them other names.

And people have changed their names to save themselves. Such was the case in some European countries and Ireland. In order to stay alive during political upheaval or war, people disclaimed their heritage and changed their names. Such circumstances deal the researcher a very difficult hand to play.

But don't overlook middle names. They can be your ace in the hole. Many times they are themselves, surnames - and can point to another stem of the family.

Now let's talk a bit about first (or given, Christian) names. They, too, can be revealing.

In the South and New England states Biblical names were popular. Female children were often given the qualities of soul or spirit. We find many girls called Faith, Sympathy, Constance, Hope, Charity and Mercy. It is not uncommon for these names to be carried from generation to generation. You may also find two children in the same family with identical names. This usually means the first died.

As you probably noticed in your research, there was an abundance of Johns, Williams, and Edwards in the late 1800's. (And very few Toms, Dicks or Harrys). Catherine, Sarah, Mary, Esther and Annie were popular names for girls during that period.

Indian children were typically dubbed with whatever their father saw just after the birth of the child. Therefore, we find Sitting Bull, Red Cloud, Spotted Tail, Rain-in-the-Face, and Little Dove.

The translation of names can also hold clues. "Silvia" is the Latin word meaning a wood. No doubt Sylvia was born in a forested area. "Peter" is Greek for rock, which may point to his habitat.

Recent studies have pinpointed some intriguing concepts about first names. It seems that a person's name has bearing on what others expect of him - and what he is like as a person.

We tend to live up to our names. This is known as the "Self-fulfilling Prophesy." Your name has power. It can give you great self-respect...or be a social albatross. It can affect your grades in school; help or hinder you in business.

Whether we like it or not, names have stereotypes. Tonys, are considered sociable, Agneses old, and Johns, trustworthy. Harveys, - unfortunately - are usually thought of as bumbling and weak. And a girl named Hortense has three strikes against her.

In general, the less unusual and complicated your first name is, the better.

As reported by Mary Marcus in the October, 1976 issue of PSYCHOLOGY TODAY, a team of U.S. psychologists asked college students to rate over 1,000 names on such points as whether they liked the name, if they thought its owner would be active or passive, and how masculine or feminine they seemed.

The students especially liked active Michael, James and Wendy. They felt Wendy must be very feminine; while the men sounded quite masculine. On the contrary, they disliked passive Alfreda, Percival and Isadore. There was a question about the masculinity of Percival and Isadore; and Alfreda's femininity was also in doubt.

The important thing here is that we can glean insight into our forebearers by thinking about their first names. Did Uncle Claude suffer from the label his parents gave him? What about your grandmother with the velvety soft name...was she indeed an ultra feminine creature?

Good references for further study on names can be found in the Library of Congress publication "Surnames: A Selected List of References." Get it free by writing General Reference and Bibliographer Division, Library of Congress, Washington DC 20540. It covers works that deal with names from such origins as: German and Swiss, Oriental, Irish, Jewish, Italian, Hispanic, Dutch, French, Belgian and British. A particularly good book on the subject is the NEW DICTIONARY OF AMERICAN FAMILY NAMES by Elsdon C. Smith.

13
Bridging the Oceans

The pride of ancestry increases in the ratio of distance.

George William Curtis

As you stalk further into the forests of your background to uncover the deepest roots, it will be necessary to probe the records in your ancestor's mother country. This isn't practical, however, until you've laid a foundation in American records. It is here you will gather the appropriate clues to guide your search abroad.

If your progenitor (direct ancestor) arrived before 1700 and was a man of property, a book called PERSONS OF QUALITY WHO CAME FROM GREAT BRITAIN TO THE AMERICAN PLANTATIONS, 1600-1700 will save you much time in tracking him down.

Knowing a bit of history helps, too. While England was the main supplier of new settlers up to the first half of the nineteenth century, Irish and German immigrants streamed in thereafter. If your great-great grandmother is Irish, chances are good she came to America sometime between 1845 and 1850 to escape the potato famine in Ireland. It was responsible for an estimated one million Irish immigrants.

Germans seeking to avoid the suppression of liberal philosophies in their homeland headed for America about the same time. Internal upheaval in a foreign country was often responsible for people journeying to the New Land.

Census records again come to the rescue when trying to bridge the Atlantic. The 1880 census noted the birthplace of a person and that of their parents. If foreign born, the 1900 census lists the year of immigration and whether naturalized. And the 1870 census showed all males over 21 who were U.S. citizens. Therefore, if an immigrant ancestor is reported as a citizen, you know there are naturalization papers - or a petition - somewhere. The petition will feed your search heartily.

Another source to consult, when you are following foreign forebearers, is the Mormon Genealogical libraries. You'll recall they have records dating back beyond 1538 and covering many different countries. And don't forget the Library of Congress and her 30,000 American and foreign genealogies and the DAR's Washington headquarters.

Passport applications may also be rich lodes. While they were not required by law, many got them to avoid being drafted into military service. Chances are, that passport leads directly to the homeland.

Military, church, land and probate records may hide more veins of gold. Also dig in obituary columns for a reference to the place of origin.

Ships' passenger lists are a vital tool, in spite of their incompleteness. Unfortunately, not all arrivals are documented. On the other hand, all <u>exits</u> from European ports are recorded.

To find source information on people who came to America before 1826, consult A BIBLIOGRAPHY OF SHIP PASSENGER LISTS, 1538-1825, compiled by Harold Lancour. It was revised and enlarged by Richard J. Wolfe in 1963.

To catch the scent of later arrivals, check your main public or research library for a copy of the MORTON ALLAN DIRECTORY OF EUROPEAN PASSENGER STEAMSHIP ARRIVALS. It lists by year, steamship company and exact date, the names of vessels arriving at New York from 1890-1930. Arrivals at Baltimore, Boston and Philadelphia from 1904 to 1926 are also catalogued in this reference volume.

Records for the port of Baltimore were created as a result of state legislation relating to immigrants. Alphabetically indexed lists of aliens who arrived at Baltimore during the years 1833 to 1866 are maintained by the city. For information write the Department of Legislative Reference, City Hall, Baltimore, Maryland 21202. Copies are also in the Mormon Salt Lake library.

The National Archives has incomplete series of customs passenger lists and immigration passenger lists of ships arriving from abroad at Atlantic and Gulf of Mexico ports. If you can provide them the name of the passenger, port of entry, vessel name and the approximate date of arrival, researchers at the Archives will check the customs passenger lists for you.

A customs passenger list normally contains each passenger's name, age, and occupation, in addition to the country of origin and country of destination. The immigration passenger lists that are 50 years old (those less than that are not open for reference purposes) will often provide the place of birth and last place of residence in addition to the above information.

Here are a couple of random points that may help you wend your way through the underbrush of immigration: Ellis Island in New York was thought of by many as the Gateway to America; while Liverpool and La Havre were the big ports of debarkation from Europe.

If you have an ancestor who became a naturalized citizen, the U.S. Immigration and Naturalization Service has records of all naturalizations that occurred after September 26, 1906. You can write them at the Department of Justice, 425 Eye Street, NW, Washington DC 20536. Make contact with your local or district office first, however, as there is a special form that should be used for inquiries. This information is also at Federal District Courts of residence or probate courts.

Proceedings of the District of Columbia

courts from 1802 to 1926 are housed in the Washington National Records Center. These records
generally show name of the new citizen, age or
date of birth, nationality, spouse and children,
date and place of arrival in the U.S.

The National Archives has photocopies and
indexes of naturalization documents from 1787 to
1906 which were filed by courts in Maine, Massachusetts, New Hampshire and Rhode Island. Before
that, immigrant arrivals were a colonial matter,
and any records would be in the original 13 colonies.

Now that you've used your genealogical pick
and shovel as much as possible on American soil,
it's time to prospect in the records offices of
the country from which your ancestors came. There
are several ways to locate them. First, try the
yellow pages of your phone directory to see if a
local consulate or foreign representative is listed for the country you're researching.

If you come up empty-handed there, call the
nearest Federal Information Center. They have
lists of embassies in Washington and a Foreign
Service List which will put you in touch with
someone who can supply the proper addresses for
various records centers. As of this writing, you
can also purchase a DIPLOMATIC LIST of foreign
embassies in the U.S. for $5.80 a year. Order
this publication from the Superintendent of
Documents, U.S. Government Printing Office, Washington DC 20402.

When you write and ask for information about
your ancestors, give them all the pertinent data
you have, especially full names and the approximate dates lived in that country. Be sure to air
mail your letter of inquiry. And it is courteous
to include a self-addressed envelope and an International Reply Coupon. This coupon, purchased
at a U.S. post office, can be turned in anywhere
in the world for that country's postage stamps.

State archives in many places in the world
own birth, marriage and death indexes that will
help locate immigrants. All you need to supply
is the name and date of birth.

For Anglo-Americans, there is a source in
England that will now trace the ancestry of
"commoners" as well as the British aristocracy.
Debrett's Peerage, Ltd. of London is the guru of
British pedigree and form. They can be reached
by writing Neville House, Eden Street, Kingston
on the Thames, England. They do not conduct free

research. For an easy-to-trace family, Debrett's will deliver eight generations for roughly $200.

"It's rather difficult to go back beyond the 15th century," comments Harold Brooks-Baker, the managing director. The numbers multiply like rabbits when you plunge deep into a line. Tracing a family back to 1600 involves about 65,000 ancestors! Some distinguished families can be tracked clear back to the 6th or 7th century, Brooks-Baker says.

Other European sources of information include: The College of Arms, London, England - Court of the Lord Lyon, Edinburgh, Scotland - Deutsche Wappenrolle, West Berlin, Germany - and Ulster Registry Office, Dublin Castle, Dublin, Ireland. Heraldic registry offices can be found in the capitals of most European countries. You can find out what the capital is by consulting THE WORLD ALMANAC.

If your heritage leads you behind the Iron Curtain into Eastern Europe, you may have some trouble finding an Achilles' heel. An amateur has little hope of getting to records here, but it can be done by a competent professional genealogist. Teams from Salt Lake had recent success filming records in East Germany, Hungary, Poland, Russia and Czechoslovakia.

Of course, one ideal way to nurture your family tree to full growth is to take a foreign vacation. What could be more exciting than to go on a pilgrimage to your ancestral village? You'll hear the shouts of robust vendors and melodious ethnic tunes. The pungent aroma of native delicacies will tease your nostrils and taste buds. Festivities rich in tradition will enchant you.

Not only are you likely to find your link with the past in old records and cemeteries, but you'll have a marvelous reason to become personally involved with some of the current local inhabitants - they are no doubt long-lost relatives!

14

Preserving Your Genealogical Trophies

The family is one of nature's masterpieces.

George Santayana

THE LIFE OF REASON, Vol. ii

You have now come to the end of your journey. What once seemed remote and mysterious is, in fact, known and within your grasp. You aren't part of a huge melting pot. Rather, you have a new personal identity - a real, living link with ethnic history - a feeling of family pride.

But just as any successful safari-goer would want photographs or mounted trophies as enduring reminders of their exciting adventure, so should you have a way to preserve your family tree.

The way to do it is to write a Family History. It isn't really hard to do. Think back to a time when you discovered a new link in your blood line. Remember the tingle of excitement that ran through you? Just let this same enthusiasm guide you when committing to paper the things you've learned. Write in short, simple sentences. Sprinkle your story with any funny incidents you dug up.

Expand the bare facts you've gathered. Paint a general narrative account based on your insights about what happened in your family. These people weren't stainless steel robots. Tell interesting anecdotes about how they lived and what they did. Sketch in their immigration from the old country and any migrations in the U.S. Tell of traditions and heirlooms passed from generation to generation. Wherever possible, include photographs to illustrate your story.

Then write one paragraph about each person. Tell what you know of his or her physical appearance, any handicaps or health problems. Show glimpses of personality and attitudes. Note occupations and avocations, membership in churches, lodges, or groups. List any unusual accomplishments or awards received. Help future readers perceive each person as a living being who dealt with the same feelings of joy and sorrow, success and failure that we experience today. Let their personal texture and color burst through.

Since you are the one creating this chronicle, a personal history of you is an important facet. Future generations will hunger to know what sort of person took the time to lovingly reconstruct The Family History. It's probably harder to write about ourselves than any other subject on earth. Yet, ironically, this is the subject about which we know the most! But vanity's skirts get in our way.

To make it easier, start with a chronological re-cap of when and where you were born. Get all the names, dates, places and relationships in your life planted. Then branch out to talk about your school days, unusual happenings, romances, vacations, holidays, and special celebrations that stand out in your mind. Tell how you feel about religion, parapsychology, and the state of the nation. Share your pleasures, your dreams, your plans. Allow the reader the ultimate privilege of seeing your essence. This is perhaps the greatest gift one person can give another.

Now use your Family Organization (see Chapter 2) to complete the picture. Solicit autobiographical material from each member to be compiled in the History. This family portrait will not only be treasured by present kin, but will have impact on unborn generations. To be lasting, however, communications to your descendants must be written. Otherwise priceless details are lost.

You can mimeograph, duplicate or print several copies of the Family History for present relatives. (Be sure and make a few extras for children to come). It's also a nice gesture to place a History in the local library, genealogical society, and historical society. And to help others in their research, why not send copies to some of the national depositories we discussed throughout DISCOVER YOUR ROOTS.

A dramatic place to distribute The History would be at your annual family reunion. As Alex

Haley says, "It is particularly important to quietly influence younger people to reflect and contribute to their families' demonstrated pride in itself."

Another way to preserve your ancestry is through membership in various hereditary and patriotic societies. The Daughters of the American Revolution (DAR) is probably the best-known of such groups. There is also the Sons of the American Revolution (SAR), the Society of Mayflower Descendants, the Society of Colonial Wars, and the Sons of Norway - to name a few. To join these organizations you must prove your lineal descent.

And finally, you may be entitled to bear a Coat of Arms. Chances of this are slim though. Technically, no matter what your surname, only the eldest son of the eldest son of families who actually bore arms is entitled to a shield. Currently, there is a flourishing trade in bogus Coats of Arms, so beware of buying decorative momentos that have no authentic value.

The Coat of Arms dates back to Greece and Rome. In ancient battles warriors were not recognizable because they were covered by armor and a helmet visor. Therefore, to identify himself a man wore a covering over his armor on which his family insignia was embroidered. This is how heraldry, which is the use of family insignia, first began. For more information about the subject, contact The Committee on Heraldry at the New England Historic Genealogy Society, 101 Newbury Street, Boston, Massachusetts 02116.

History is a combination of geography and biography. It has been said that by examining the lives of remote cousins or the land of great-great-great-great grandparents, descendants can find a usable past that no map or textbook can communicate.

You've made that examination. As an amateur genealogist, you've used the nose of a bloodhound, the cleverness of a fox and the persistence of an elephant to ferret out a family legacy. Hopefully, it's been a happy and successful hunt.

now you can have your very own

"PERSONALIZED" FAMILY TREE FOLIO

This unique package includes 15 handy PERSONAL
PROFILE SHEETS to make your genealogical search
easier. These forms are designed to capture all
the fascinating details about each of your ancestors. They come in a beautiful and functional
folder, "Personalized" with your family surname.

Not only are they a useful tool, when completed
by you, they MAKE IDEAL GIFTS FOR FAMILY MEMBERS.
The complete folio is only $3.95.

S p e c i a l B o n u s :
Included at no extra cost, we will supply you
with a current list of all Federal Information
Centers and their free telephone tielines.

(ORDER FORM FOR "PERSONALIZED" FAMILY TREE FOLIO)

Please send me ____ folio(s) at $3.95 each. I
have enclosed $____ (California residents add
24¢ for each folio.) Please print clearly!

FAMILY SURNAME DESIRED_____

YOUR NAME _____

ADDRESS _____

CITY & STATE _____ZIP_____

Make check payable to: COMMUNICATION CREATIVITY
P.O. Box 17120, San Diego, California 92117

Send a copy of DISCOVER YOUR ROOTS to a friend

Please send _____ copies of DISCOVER YOUR ROOTS
at $4.95 each.
I've enclosed $_____(California residents add
sales tax of 30¢ for each book.) Please print.

SEND TO _____

ADDRESS _____

CITY & STATE _____ZIP_____

SIGN THE GIFT CARD _____

Make check payable to: COMMUNICATION CREATIVITY,
P.O. Box 17120, San Diego, California 92117

NATIONAL ARCHIVES AND RECORDS SERVICE
Locations and Areas Served

Appendix A

Headquarters
Central Reference Division
7th and Pennsylvania Avenue N.W.
Washington, D.C. 20408
(Telephone: 202/523-3218; hours:
8:45 a.m.-9:45 p.m., Mon.-Fri.;
9:00 a.m.-5:00 p.m., Sat.)

Atlanta
1557 St. Joseph Ave.
East Point, Ga. 30344
(Telephone: 404/526-7477; hours:
8:00 a.m.-4:30 p.m., Mon.-Fri. Serves
Alabama, Georgia, Florida, Kentucky,
Mississippi, North Carolina, South
Carolina, and Tennessee.)

Boston
380 Trapelo Rd.
Waltham, Mass. 02154
(Telephone: 817/223-2657; hours: 8 a.m.-
4:30 p.m., Mon.-Fri. Serves Connecticut,
Maine, Massachusetts, New Hampshire,
Rhode Island, and Vermont.)

Chicago
7358 S. Pulaski Rd.
Chicago, Illinois 60629
(Telephone: 312/353-8541; hours:
8:00 a.m.-4:30 p.m., Mon.-Fri. Serves
Illinois, Indiana, Michigan, Minnesota,
Ohio, and Wisconsin.)

Denver
Building 48, Denver Federal Center
Denver, Colo. 80225
(Telephone: 303/234-5271; hours:
7:30 a.m.-4:00 p.m., Mon.-Fri. Serves
Colorado, Montana, North Dakota,
South Dakota, Utah, and Wyoming.)

Fort Worth
4900 Hemphill St. (building address)
P. O. Box 6216 (mailing address)
Fort Worth, Tex. 76115
(Telephone: 817/334-5515; hours:
8:00 a.m.-4:30 p.m., Mon.-Fri. Serves
Arkansas, Louisiana, New Mexico,
Oklahoma, and Texas.)

Kansas City
2306 E. Bannister Rd.
Kansas City, Mo. 64131
(Telephone: 816/926-7271; hours:
8:00 a.m.-4:30 p.m., Mon.-Fri. Serves
Iowa, Kansas, Missouri, and Nebraska.)

Los Angeles
24000 Avila Rd.
Laguna Niguel, Calif. 92677
(Telephone: 714/831-4220; hours:
8:00 a.m.-4:30 p.m., Mon.-Fri. Serves
Arizona, the southern California counties
of Imperial, Inyo, Kern, Los Angeles,
Orange, Riverside, San Bernardino, San
Diego, San Luis Obispo, Santa Barbara,
and Ventura; and Clark County, Nev.)

New York
Building 22—MOT Bayonne
Bayonne, N.J. 07002
(Telephone: 201/858-7245; hours: 8 a.m.-
5:00 p.m., Mon.-Fri. Serves New Jersey,
New York, Puerto Rico, and the Virgin
Islands.)

Philadelphia
5000 Wissahickon Ave.
Philadelphia, Pa. 19144
(Telephone: 214/438-5200, ext. 591;
hours: 8:00 a.m.-4:30 p.m., Mon.-Fri.
Serves Delaware and Pennsylvania; for the
loan of microfilm, also serves the District
of Columbia, Maryland, Virginia, and
West Virginia.)

San Francisco
1000 Commodore Dr.
San Bruno, Calif. 94066
(Telephone: 415/876-9001; hours:
7:45 a.m.-4:15 p.m., Mon.-Fri. Serves
California (except southern California),
Hawaii, Nevada (except Clark County),
and the Pacific Ocean area.)

Seattle
6125 Sand Point Way NE
Seattle, Wash. 98115
(Telephone: 206/442-4502; hours:
8:00 a.m.-4:30 p.m., Mon.-Fri. Serves
Alaska, Idaho, Oregon, and Washington.)

Includes supplemental schedules open to the public

B

1790

Name of family head; free white males of 16 years and up, free white males under 16; free white females; slaves; other persons.

1800

Name of family head; if white, age and sex; race; slaves.

1810

Name of family head; if white, age and sex; race; slaves.

1820

Name of family head; age; sex; race; foreigners not naturalized; slaves; industry (agriculture, commerce, and manufactures).

1830

Name of family head; age; sex; race; slaves; deaf and dumb; blind; foreigners not naturalized.

1840

Name of family head; age; sex; race; slaves; number of deaf and dumb; number of blind; number of insane and idiotic and whether in public or private charge; number of persons in each family employed in each of six classes of industry and one of occupation; literacy; pensioners for Revolutionary or military service.

1850

Name; age; sex; race; whether deaf and dumb, blind, insane, or idiotic; value of real estate; occupation; birthplace; whether married within the year; school attendance; literacy; whether a pauper or convict.

Supplemental schedules for slaves; public paupers and criminals; persons who died during the year.

1860

Name; age; sex; race; value of real estate; value of personal estate; occupation; birthplace; whether married within the year; school attendance; literacy; whether deaf and dumb; blind, insane, idiotic, pauper, or convict; number of slave houses.

Supplemental schedules for slaves; public paupers and criminals; persons who died during the year.

1870

Name; age; race; occupation; value of real estate; value of personal estate; birthplace; whether parents were foreign born; month of birth if born within the year; month of marriage if married within the year; school attendance; literacy; whether deaf and dumb, blind, insane, or idiotic; male citizens 21 and over, and number of such persons denied the right to vote for other than rebellion.

Supplemental schedules for persons who died during the year; paupers; prisoners.

1880

Address; name; relationship to family head; sex; race; age; marital status; month of birth if born within the census year; occupation; months unemployed during the year; sickness or temporary disability; whether blind, deaf and dumb, idiotic, insane, maimed, crippled, bedridden, or otherwise disabled; school attendance; literacy; birthplace of person and parents.

Supplemental schedules for the Indian population; for persons who died during the year; insane; idiots; deaf-mutes; blind; homeless children; prisoners; paupers and indigent persons.

1890

(schedules destroyed)

1900

Address; name; relationship to family head; sex; race; age; marital status; number of years married; for women, number of children born and number now living; birthplace of person and parents; if foreign born, year of immigration and whether naturalized; occupation; months not employed; school attendance; literacy; ability to speak English; whether on a farm; home owned or rented and if owned, whether mortgaged.

Supplemental schedules for the blind and for the deaf.

1910

Address; name; relationship to family head; sex; race; age; marital status; number of years of present marriage; for women, number of children born and number now living; birthplace and mother tongue of person and parents; if foreign born, year of immigration, whether naturalized, and whether able to speak English, or if not, language spoken; occupation, industry, and class of worker; if an employee, whether out of work during year; literacy; school attendance; home owned or rented; if owned, whether mortgaged; whether farm or house; whether a survivor of Union or Confederate Army or Navy; whether blind or deaf and dumb

1920

Address; name; relationship to family head; sex; race; age; marital status; if foreign born, year of immigration to the U.S., whether naturalized, and year of naturalization; school attendance; literacy; birthplace of person and parents; mother tongue of foreign born; ability to speak English; occupation, industry, and class of worker; home owned or rented; if owned, whether mortgaged; for nonfarm mortgaged, market value, original amount of mortgage, balance due, interest rate.

1930

Address; name; relationship to family head; home owned or rented; value or monthly rental; radio set; whether on a farm; sex; race; age; marital status; age at first marriage; school attendance; literacy; birthplace of person and parents; if foreign born, language spoken in home before coming to U.S., year of immigration, whether naturalized, and ability to speak English; occupation, industry, and class of worker; whether at work previous day (or last regular working day); veteran status; for Indians, whether of full or mixed blood, and tribal affiliation.

1940

Address; home owned or rented; value or monthly rental; whether on a farm; relationship to household head; sex; race; age; marital status; school attendance; educational attainment; birthplace; citizenship of foreign born; location of residence 5 years ago and whether on a farm; employment status; if at work, whether in private or nonemergency government work, or in public emergency work (WPA, CCC, NYA, etc.); if in private or nonemergency government work, hours worked in week; if seeking work or on public emergency work, duration of unemployment; occupation, industry, and class of worker; weeks worked last year; income last year.

1950

Address; whether house is on farm; name; relationship to household head; race; sex; age; marital status; birthplace; if foreign born, whether naturalized; employment status; hours worked in week; occupation, industry, and class of worker.

1960 and 1970

Address; name; relationship to household head; sex; race; age; marital status.

C

GENEALOGY: A SELECTED BIBLIOGRAPHY by Milton Rubicam, C.G., F.A.S.G. (3rd rev. ed.) Institute of Genealogical & Historical Research, Samford University Library, Birmingham, Ala. 35209.

GUIDE TO GENEALOGICAL RECORDS IN THE NATIONAL ARCHIVES. Superintendent of Documents, U.S. Government Printing Office, Washington, DC 20402.

(THE) HANDY BOOK FOR GENEALOGISTS by George B. Everton, Sr. Everton Publishers, Inc.

HOW TO TRACE YOUR FAMILY TREE by the American Genealogical Research Institute Staff, Dolphin Books.

(THE) RESEARCHER'S GUIDE TO AMERICAN GENEALOGY by Val D. Greenwood. Genealogical Publishing Co., 521-523 St. Paul Pl., Baltimore, Md. 21202.

SEARCHING FOR YOUR ANCESTORS: THE HOW AND WHY OF GENEALOGY by Gilbert H. Doane, F.A.S.G. Banton Book Co.

Addresses noted for those publications not easily obtained at bookstores.

INDEX

Index